Surviving Formula One Withdrawal

From Abu Dhabi to Melbourne

Techniques Every F1 Fan Needs To Know To Be the Best They Can Possibly Be

By J S Eton

(with Molly Petrol Head)

This book is dedicated to

F1 fans around the world

and their long suffering families.

For Mum, Dad, Alan and

Chief Race Engineer, Lisa

Love Always

Eets

Table of Contents

Attention: A Special Note About How This Book Was Created

Dear Formula One Fan,

Thank you for claiming your copy of

"Surviving Formula One Withdrawal from Abu Dhabi To Melbourne: Techniques Every F1 Fan Needs To Know To Be the Best They Can Possibly Be".

This book will teach you the skills, tools, techniques, and more that every Formula One fan should understand to make the most of the break and to successfully survive F1 withdrawal—all in a readable, light-hearted way.

This book was originally created as a live interview.

That's why the book <u>reads like a conversation</u> rather than like a traditional "book" that talks "at" you.

I wanted you to feel as though I were talking "with" you, like a friend would.

I felt that crafting the narrative in this way would make it easier for you to review the topics and to put them to use quickly, rather than wading through hundreds of pages to get to the point. This way, we can get straight to the crucial information.

So, relax. Grab a pen and some paper to note your thoughts and ideas as you read.

Get ready to take your survival of Formula One withdrawal to the next level.

Let's get started by considering various techniques to survive F1 withdrawal from Abu Dhabi to Melbourne—from one season to the next. You'll learn how to overcome your fears, and you'll be encouraged to experiment with these and many more ideas and opportunities for self-growth.

Enjoy! The world awaits—explore it, and be the best that you can be.

J S Eton

Introduction – Surviving Formula One Withdrawal from Abu Dhabi to Melbourne

"Ambition is putting a ladder against the sky."

Anonymous

MPH: Hello, everyone, and welcome to "Surviving Formula One Withdrawal from Abu Dhabi To Melbourne: Techniques Every F1 Fan Needs To Know To Be the Best They Can Possibly Be"

My name is Molly Petrol Head, and today I'm talking with J S Eton about various techniques that could help you to survive F1 withdrawal from one season to the next.

By the end of this interview, you'll understand how to overcome your fears, and will be inspired to experiment with new ideas and opportunities to truly be the best that you can be.

Welcome J S Eton!

JSE: Thanks, Molly—great to be here. Thank you for inviting me.

MPH: J S Eton is an expert on the subject of surviving Formula One withdrawal, and has graciously consented to this interview to share extensive knowledge and experience. J S Eton hopes that, by the end of this interview, every Formula One fan will understand:

- How to effectively handle F1 withdrawal
- How to improve your life with family and friends without locking up
- How to improve your bodywork and get circuit-ready
- How to improve your fuel consumption and ace your food choices
- How to face your fears and push through the pit wall to be the best that you can be

J S Eton, thank you again for joining us on this live interview.

JSE: My pleasure. I'm looking forward to our time together today.

Chapter One: The Rules of the Road

"We must take adventures in order to know where we truly belong."

Anonymous

MPH: Let's jump right in so that you can share your thoughts about surviving Formula One withdrawal. Could you tell us a little about yourself—what is your background, education, and experience surviving Formula One withdrawal? When did you get started? Have you had any formal training or education in surviving Formula One withdrawal, or is your knowledge primarily experience-based? Why have you chosen to share your knowledge here with us?

JSE: Of course. From an educational perspective, I've a Master's of Science degree. I received my formal survival training from the school of life, when it comes to F1.

I have studied psychology extensively over the years, and I've observed the impact of various scenarios and stresses on people. I've also had the privilege to coach and mentor people to overcome their greatest fears and challenges, and to help them realise their true potential.

In terms of my F1 withdrawal experience, this all began in 2015 whilst watching the Abu Dhabi GP in Australia. Some of my friends were at the actual circuit, watching from the hill, and they saw Nico win the race. Lewis, had already secured the Championship, in Austin at the United States Grand Prix.

When the race ended, it was very late in Australia, and I was alone—everyone else had gone to bed. I recall thinking, *What now?* The rest is history. So, why this book? I'd simply like to help other people, and to share my experiences.

We all know what it's like—the season ends, and suddenly, you face a massive void of time. The spike in withdrawal symptoms after the recent World Cup has been fascinating to watch—it's not uncommon for avid fans to really feel the void.

Clearly, F1 withdrawal is far more severe than any football withdrawal—not that I'm biased in any way.

Often, the world takes itself far too seriously, and so this book takes a hybrid approach. It offers an honest look at activities that can help you to survive from one season to the next, and to have some fun along the way.

MPH: I'm with you on the F1 withdrawal. Thank you for sharing. I'm excited! What kinds of things have you done and what experiences have you had surviving Formula One withdrawal that are relevant to our audience?

JSE: That's a great question. Over the last few years, I've tried a number of remedies to this withdrawal, and have had some fantastic experiences. Some have been more successful than others—more on that later. These remedies have included:

- Reconnecting with family and friends
- Getting fit
- Finding the kitchen and learning to cook
- Compiling a "Bucket List"
- Watching movies and box sets
- Travelling (seeing penguins, pandas, and hot air balloons)
- Learning to speak other languages
- Decluttering
- Gardening, meditating, and breathing that clear air
- Reading books and listening to audiobooks (and writing one!)

- Developing playlists to match my mood
- Hosting an F1 championship
- Developing fan pages and fantasy GP leagues
- Kicking a bad habit and creating a new habit
- Shopping for pre-season essentials
- Other interesting stuff!

MPH: Wow! That's fantastic. Can we explore this in more detail? I love penguins. I can't wait to hear that story, along with many others.

JSE: Sure, no problem. The most important thing to remember is that, depending upon the calendar, there are approximately 15 weeks to fill between the end of the F1 Championship in Abu Dhabi and the commencement in Melbourne of the new season.

MPH: OK, that's a long time! I wouldn't know where to start. In your experience, how have you effectively handled F1 withdrawal?

JSE: We're all different, and so what's right for one person may be different from what's right for another. That's what makes life interesting. The key thing for me, personally, is staying busy and having a rough idea or a plan of the things that I want to do.

For example, how many times when you've been on holiday have you seen most of the things you wanted to see, relaxed, and ate at the restaurants you wanted to visit?

Yet, when a friend comes to visit and asks about the local restaurants or nearby places of interest, you find yourself saying, "Oh yes, there's a new restaurant that we've been meaning to check out," only to discover that it's been open for over a year!

MPH: Yes, that's so true! I can definitely relate to that. I actually had that experience a few months ago with a friend who was visiting from Spain, and rather embarrassingly, it was a tapas restaurant!

JSE: Oh, OK. In life, we tend to just "go with the flow." We undertake our routines, get up, shower, get dressed, go to work, come home, make dinner, clean up, and then it's time to sleep. Sometimes, life just seems to take over.

The following day, we get up and repeat the cycle. Unless you make time to decide what you want to do, it may never happen.

MPH: I agree! That certainly sounds like me and my family.

JSE: The purpose of this book isn't to provide a comprehensive thesis on each idea. I could probably write a book on each topic in its own right! Instead, the book is meant to provide an overview of each topic, and if people are interested in that particular topic, they'll naturally explore it further.

MPH: I'm in for more books!

JSE: (Laughs) Well, let's get started on this one, and we'll see what happens! The public will decide.

OK, so Abu Dhabi has finished, and the Championship is over.

Now is your time— you have 15 weeks to fill.

Life is waiting—get out of that pit lane. Decide to go for it!

Chapter Two: The #1 Rule of Surviving F1 Withdrawal That You Should Never Break

"When all else fails, follow instructions."

Anonymous

MPH: OK, let's stay on the theme of taking action. What's the #1 rule that Formula One fans should follow to successfully survive Formula One withdrawal?

JSE: That's a great question. I'm not often serious, but in my experience, you have to make a fundamental decision—ideally, just before the end of the season. The question is—F1 or no F1? Once you decide, you can't change your decision.

Most of us have experienced the post-holiday blues, or the guilt of committing to give something up and breaking our commitment. This situation is no different. When we do something we like, dopamine is released in the brain. Dopamine is a neurotransmitter that supports the brain's response to reward and motivation. This makes us feel pleasure and excitement.

Once the season is over, die-hard fans may face a significant emotional low. The lack of dopamine can also contribute to irritability and can impact our mood. In extreme cases, the "duvet days" may commence, when you feel you have no reason to get out of bed, and your alcohol, junk food, or ice cream consumption may also increase.

So, which way do you go—do you check out for these 15 weeks, or do you stay checked in?

The decision is a personal one, as we are all different, and our ideal responses are different. In either case, you can still count the weeks, days, hours, minutes, and seconds until the start of the next season, if that's going to help you.

Decision Point:

- A. Stay checked into F1: F1 remains a constant in your life. You remain current with the latest news and developments in the sport.
- B. Check out of F1: Complete break from F1 (cold turkey). You temporarily remove F1 from your life as you explore other activities and opportunities. They do say that absence makes the heart grow fonder.

MPH: That's fascinating, and it makes a lot of sense. Can I ask what happens if you break the rule?

JSE: Sure. I would encourage you to remind yourself why you made that decision in the first place, as you made that decision for a reason. Sharing your intentions with family and friends is another helpful method, as they can support you on your journey. Also, public commitments are harder to walk away from!

In a way, this question is similar to asking what happens if you decide to get fit, go on a diet, or quit a habit, and you break your commitment. It's not the end of the world, but quite simply, you directly feel the impact mentally, emotionally, and physically.

You'll simply not achieve what you set out to achieve.

My advice is to make a firm decision, enjoy, and have fun, but stay on the (pit) straight and narrow.

Chapter Three: Techniques to Successfully Survive Formula One Withdrawal

"This life is your gift to yourself, open it!"

Anonymous

MPH: Thank you. My next questions concern what's next, and the techniques you've proposed. So, once Formula One fans make their decision, what's next? Is there anything that you think may help fans make their decision, if they're still undecided? What are your recommendations for techniques? And when does it all start?

JSE: I'll deal with the question of indecision first. There are several techniques I've used in the past for making decisions. Some examples include the "five whys," a simple analysis of pros and cons, or a more detailed tool—this is getting serious—bring on the spreadsheet wizardry.

Five "Whys" – Grab a piece of paper, and draw two equal columns and six rows. In the top row, simply note the two headers, which should be checked "in" and "out." Next, take each column in turn.

Ask yourself—why do you want to stay checked in? Note your answer in the first row, then consider why you made the decision you've just documented. Continue this process until you've populated the table.

Then, review the two columns, compare them, and decide what will work best for you.

Simple List of Pros and Cons – Grab a piece of paper, and draw two columns. Next, draw two more columns within each column. Note the two headers checked "in" and "out" at the top level, and add a + and – sign at the top of each subsection. Note the positives and negatives of each of the two scenarios for you personally.

Then, review the two columns, and decide what will work best for you.

Spreadsheet! – This really is the "big guns." You could always get quite analytical if you wish, and plot your two options on the x axis, and the elements that are important to you on the y axis.

Complete your answers, and if you are so inclined, you can also assign points and add weights to each element, dependent upon their importance.

Alternatively, you can toss a coin. That's what's cool about this method – it's *your* call entirely.

So, once you've made your decision, your immediate actions are:

Checked In	Checked Out (Cold Turkey)
Review all the World Championship social media and footage from Abu Dhabi.	Review all social media for F1-related apps and news, and turn off all notifications.
Read chapters 4-13 of this book, and highlight the activities you're interested in.	Review your apps and download / refresh news and other areas of interest.
Prioritise the activities you've highlighted, and decide what you'd like to do.	Read chapters 4-13 of this book, prioritise and decide what you'd like to do.
Let those close to you know your plans over the break, and understand their appetite to be involved.	

In terms of techniques, over the following circuits (sorry, chapters) you'll gain a taste of the differing activities and experiences that you can try over the break. You may decide simply to focus on one activity; alternatively, you may choose a different activity each week. That's entirely up to you.

In terms of your final question, Molly, it all starts at 00:00 hours on the day of the final race of the season.

Chapter Four: Improve Your Life with Family and Friends Without Locking Up

"Family, our refuge from the storm, our link to the past, and our bridge to the future."

Anonymous

MPH: That's really helpful—thank you. As you said earlier, let's get into the techniques. What advice can you offer Formula One fans to improve their relationships with their family and friends without locking up?

JSE: OK, so this is one of my favourite ways to spend part of the break. Your level of passion for F1 may impact how challenging this is for you.

If you've been a little distracted by the Championship (possibly by being absent for almost 21 weekends), this could be interesting! Go and take a walk around the house, or visit family and friends, and re-introduce yourself. It's important to do this both at the beginning of the break and towards the end, just before the new season gets underway. This is the best way to stay connected with your family and friends if you're planning to do some of the other activities listed in this book.

It's important to keep your perspective, and if you haven't been around to undertake jobs that needed to be done, focus on those first, so that you can truly relax when these tasks are completed and out of the way.

My other key element of advice is to use your ears and mouth in proportion—listening twice as much as you speak—especially with the people you're closest to. Catch up! Find out what's been going on in their lives, and see how you can interact with them over the coming weeks, noting key events, and get these locked into your diary.

MPH: I really like that—using the ears and mouth in proportion. It's so true, and perhaps we don't do that enough. Is there anything else you'd recommend to all F1 fans?

JSE: I agree. This connects to our earlier discussion—life is so busy and full now that it can be quite relentless, thinking about all the things to be done, both from a professional and personal perspective. Often, we just need to create the time and space to do something differently.

In terms of other activities, dig out your emergency chairs, get out the board games, gather your family and friends around, and have some fun—just spend time doing things you enjoy with those you care about. Other ideas for activities include:

Nature Walk/Park	Theme Park	Baking
Cinema/ Theatre	Bowling	Decluttering
Camping	Card Games	DIY Paint Party
Karting	Visiting Local City	Trampolining
Meal Out/In	Museum	Football
Indoor Skiing	Horse Riding	Swimming
Roller Skating	Journaling	Flying a Kite

Alternatively, a weekend away is always a good way to have quality time together.

MPH: There really are so many possibilities, as you say—and we generally don't make the time. What do you mean when you say "locking up"? And what should F1 fans do if they find themselves locking up?

JSE: Good question, Molly. "Locking up" is fairly common in F1, especially when the front wheel is going into a turn. Effectively, this means that the tyre has stopped spinning, and is sliding instead. This occurs when the driver brakes too hard.

In social situations, to "lock up" means to freeze or feel uncomfortable, perhaps not knowing what to say or do. This can occur for many reasons—perhaps if you have committed to doing something but haven't done it (naughty step scenario). Clearly, there will be a good reason as to why you've "locked up."

It could be a social gathering where your conversant knows very little about you—therefore, it's natural for them to kick start a conversation with F1 (stranger territory).

In my experience, especially if I've checked out of F1 for the break, it can be difficult for your social circle if they are used to discussing F1 with you—it can create a conversational void, and can be slightly awkward (common ground).

I'd encourage you to be open and deal with the specific scenario—just take control, be confident, and respond. For example:

- **Naughty Step** – Just own it. Acknowledge that what you committed to do hasn't been done, and describe your plans to sort it. Then, ensure that you create the time and space to complete the task, if need be. I know that it may be difficult, or near impossible for some—but just apologise. You've screwed up, so just deal with it, call it out, and move on.

- **Stranger Territory** – Be up front, and explain that F1 is a real passion—it is your first love after all—but that you're on a break until the start of the next season. I'd encourage you to keep up-to-date on current affairs and things of interest—it's ok, you aren't cheating. You are simply being more balanced with your interests, and, let's face it, as soon as that season starts, those notifications will be **ON**.

- **Common Ground** – This is similar to "stranger territory." The only exception is that you know this person well, so just go with the flow. Tell your friend about your situation, and focus on them and all the other things that you have in common.

My final thought in this chapter is that, if possible, you should try to get ahead of things that need to be done, either for you or for others, within the first few weeks or months of the new season.

This will enable you to immerse yourself in the new Championship without being on the naughty step, and to catch up on activities that have occurred over the break.

Chapter Five: Improve your Bodywork and Get Circuit-Ready

"An ounce of prevention is worth a pound of cure."

Anonymous

MPH: That's a really good tip. I like that. OK, let's move on. I know that you want to cover fitness next. How can F1 fans improve their bodywork and get circuit-ready?

JSE: This is where the excuses tend to kick in! The key question for all fans is—how is your bodywork? Are you happy? If so, then feel free to move to the next chapter. Would you like to be ripped in 15 weeks? Or bikini ready? Or, perhaps, you'd like to focus on limiting your drinking or your nibbles arm, and doing some light weights. The key is to decide what's right for you, and to set your goal for these 15 weeks.

I'll share my secret from last year's break. These are the 10 exercises I alternated to get myself circuit-ready for Melbourne—which also happened to be my birthday weekend.

10 Exercises to Give You the Most Traction

1. Ballast – Perform basic weight-lifting exercises, alternating left and right, with five raises in each set. If you don't own any weights—no problem. Start with a tin of tomatoes.
2. Blistering – Perform a low squat (as low as you can go) and move your arms behind your back, then bring them to the front, keeping them as wide as possible.

3. Backmarker – Perform five squats per set with a break of ten seconds between sets. Simply keep your back straight and move to a seated position. For an extra challenge, hold the position for five seconds once in the seated position.
4. Brake Balance – Hold your arms out to the side whilst standing on one leg. Push the foot of the other leg against the side of your standing leg to give more strength. Break for ten seconds, and then repeat with your other leg.
5. Box, Box, Box – Jog on the spot, sparring forward and performing five punches with the left hand, and then repeat the set with the right hand, with a break of twenty seconds between spars.
6. Formation Lap – Sprint as quickly as you can around your block. If training with others, the top tip scenario is to get into their slip stream. If you'd like your formation lap with a twist, sprint as quickly as you can whilst standing in the pit lane (standing still).
7. Jump Start – These are also known as jumping jacks. Start with your feet together and your arms by your side, and jump to the X position, arms and feet apart.
8. Plank – Hold a push-up position, leaning on your forearms. If you'd like your plank with a twist, roll onto your back, move to a semi-seated position, and hold. Gradually increase your hold time as you progress, beginning with five seconds.
9. Pole Positions – Hold your arms extended straight in front of your body, and alternate straight-leg raises.
10. Spinning Wheels (Donuts) – Rotate your arms forward in a circular motion, and repeat by rotating your arms backwards, still creating circles. For an extra challenge, walk on the spot whilst spinning those wheels.

MPH: That's outstanding! I can't wait to try some of those exercises. I'm loving the names you've chosen. I think that we all have good intentions, and as you rightly say, we inevitably end up running out of time or finding excuses not to take care of our bodies. What advice can you give F1 fans who want to stay focussed on their goals?

JSE: I'd encourage them to note their goals somewhere visible – that really worked for me. Then, they should monitor their progress against their goals. This could be as simple as a week-by-week progress of weight loss, or of body measurements, as the bodywork becomes more toned. Alternatively, it could be as complicated as a pit wall with key stats, analytics, and trends. The priority is to use the measurement as motivation, and to not let analytics become the priority such that the workout comes second!

MPH: Are you speaking from bad personal experience, by any chance?

JSE: (Laughs) You got me, Molly! Yes. I've definitely done that, and I've even spent valuable time recalculating how I could get back on track, and then re-forecasting that forecast when I didn't achieve it! I've learnt the hard way to just take some action.

Taking action is the most important thing. Just get out there and do something.

Every step is a move in the right direction – otherwise, you're simply standing still.

Chapter Six: Improve Your Fuel Consumption and Ace Your Food Choices

The best way to gain self-confidence is to do what you are afraid to do.

Anonymous

MPH: Our next chapter is about one of my favourite subjects. What has been your experience with food, and how can F1 fans benefit from acing their food choices?

JSE: I totally agree—it doesn't take much to distract me when food is concerned. It's a fascinating topic, because we're all different, and we all have different approaches. Some people eat for pleasure, whilst for others, eating is simply a function of survival.

MPH: Absolutely—that's so true. I love to cook, and I will happily spend hours in the kitchen each evening preparing dinner. What does food mean to you?

JSE: That's a great question—how long do we have? I tend to think in pictures, and I like to simplify things. Think of your body as a car, and the food we consume as the fuel. If you put diesel into an unleaded car, you know what the result will be! In my experience, it's all about achieving balance. Everything is fine in moderation. I personally wouldn't be happy living off celery alone, but I wouldn't judge anyone who makes that personal choice! A balanced diet is key in my experience.

MPH: That's a great analogy. I like that.

JSE: OK, Molly, that's great. Now it's time for us to find that kitchen and get cooking. On a serious note, its confession time. I have to be honest—when I first started on this journey during one of my first breaks, my kitchen skills were somewhat limited. I was reasonably good at cooking eggs. I could have made you scrambled eggs one night, and dippy egg and soldiers (toast) the second, but fried eggs were a bit hit-and-miss, so I'd not have chanced those. I do value your life. Then, there was a real outbreak of morale – beans on toast for the third night. That was probably my limit.

MPH: (Laughs) That's funny. Thank you for being so open with us.

JSE: Thankfully, I'm blessed to have a close friend who is my opposite in many ways, especially in the kitchen!

She is very patient, and was kind enough to make me a recipe book that was designed to challenge me in the kitchen. Let's be honest—my starting position on the grid left a lot to be desired. The book was comprised of various nibbles, starters, mains, and desserts.

MPH: Wow, that's a great gift idea—I really like that.

JSE: I've spent many hours working through the recipe book and creating various masterpieces and, in the very beginning, disaster-pieces! But only when I was unsupervised. We all have to start somewhere.

There is an entire industry devoted to helping you in the kitchen. You'll find a plethora of websites and books on food and food choices, and the choice you make is very much an individual preference. We all have our own habits and quirkiness.

Lewis is a great example—he enjoys a plant-based diet, and looks and feels great as a result of that personal choice.

My advice would be to experiment. If you don't already have herbs and spices in the kitchen, go for it—visit your local store or market, and purchase the basics.

MPH: What basics would you recommend?

JSE: In order to get the best flavour, if you don't already have these spices, I'd recommend buying good-quality salt and peppercorns (use the mills and you'll never go back). I'd also encourage fans to buy a pestle and mortar. Here are the spices that I use most often in the kitchen:

Basil	Garam Masala	Rosemary
Bay Leaves	Garlic Powder	Saffron
Cardamom	Ginger	Sage
Chilli Powder and Flakes (Hot)	Mixed Spices (Whole)	Star Anise
Cloves	Nutmeg	Tarragon
Cumin	Oregano	Thyme
Curry Powder	Paprika	Turmeric

MPH: I definitely have some of those in my cabinets, but I will look to expand my selection. I've not heard of star anise before. What is it?

JSE: Star Anise is a lovely spice that has a liquorice flavour. It originated in southern China, although it is also cultivated in the Philippines, Japan, and Taiwan. It's used frequently in Asian cooking, but is also used in Western cooking, and is good for sauces. I use it in a number of my favourite recipes. I've looked into sharing these recipes, but unfortunately, they are copyrighted. That's not a road that's open to us. The red flags are most certainly out.

MPH: OK, that's interesting. Yes, I understand about the copyright. Just talking about this is making me hungry! I want to dust off my recipe books at home and, as you say, start to experiment.

JSE: Exactly. Start to work through some new recipes. It's always good fun to do this with other people, and you'll learn quickly from their experience. Sometimes, they can boost your confidence when you don't feel confident in the kitchen.

I'd therefore encourage fans to do a little research into the food they enjoy, and to take that plunge and just start cooking. Amazon is always a good place to start looking if you don't have any recipes at all, although there are many other reputable stores and marketplaces.

There are also some excellent websites with free recipes just waiting to be tested and explored—so get to it.

I'd also urge fans to host some practice sessions with the snacks and nibbles you plan to indulge in during the races, although it's OK if you don't have time for this.

Remember that throughout the season, some races will be held at breakfast time, some in mid-afternoon, some in the evening, and some even during the night, depending upon your location. Some of my favourite racing snacks include:

- Home-made nachos with various toppings (I make some with and some without the heat of chili peppers for my friends with heat-resistant mouths).
- Healthy brownies (yes, I did say healthy) that are frozen rather than baked—I make these from dates, nuts, almond flour, and cocoa powder, with honey for the topping. These are ideal for breakfast-time races.

- Homemade spicy nuts (cashews with paprika and other spices baked in the oven).
- Sweet potato wedges (jackets on!). Season the sweet potatoes well, cut them into wedges, and pop them on a baking tray and straight into the oven. Remove and enjoy!
- Chicken or beef fajitas complete with home-made guacamole, salsa, and sour cream.

If I can have success in the kitchen, anyone can. You won't even need DRS. Just go for it.

What do you have to lose?

My final point on this topic is that you should balance your time in the kitchen with your other activities. If you've decided to focus on your bodywork, you may want to seek out nutritious recipes and foods that are targeted to assist with your exercise recovery and to help muscle repair. Alternatively, you may want to work hard, eat well, and play hard!

Your main driver should be discovering the routine that best fits with your personal goals.

Chapter Seven: The Championship of Life – Create your Circuits

If you imagine it, you can achieve it. If you can dream it, you can become it.

Anonymous

MPH: Excellent advice. I know that neither of us wants to leave the subject of food, but I know that you want to cover more activities for the fans. What would you like to discuss next?

JSE: You're right. I'd like to turn to the "Championship of Life." By this, I mean the things that we want to do or see in our lifetime—our "Bucket List." I know that this may sound a bit deep for some, but it's not meant to be too serious. Nor is it meant to be depressing!

Earlier, we discussed how life just happens, and how time seems to pass quickly from one year to the next.

MPH: Oh, OK. What do you mean by a "Bucket List"? Forgive me, but I've only heard that term used in the context of people with terminal illnesses. I'm open minded, but I don't have a Bucket List. Do you have one?

JSE: Yes, you're right. That's a good point. But let me be clear—you don't have to be ill to have a Bucket List!

If the term "Bucket List" feels uncomfortable, you can call it a Dream List, a Goal List, or a list of things to achieve by a certain date or age. Whatever terminology feels right for you works for me.

The Bucket List is essentially a list of things that you'd like to achieve, things you'd like to experience, places you'd like to visit, and people you'd like to see.

I volunteered for approximately five years, and during that time I met many inspirational people who coped with various life challenges, and some of whom were terminally ill.

Not one person said, "Oh, I'd like to have spent more time working, playing the PlayStation, sleeping, in the pub, or watching TV!" These people shared with me the activities they wished that they had done, the people they wished that they'd made more time for— often their children and parents—and the places they wished that they had visited when they had the opportunity. Time was always a constant excuse—"I was too busy, and I needed to do x, y, and z." So, I say, make time to do it NOW!

Writing a list inspires and empowers you. The point of making the list now is to be in a position to complete the items on your list.

I encourage everyone to make a list of the things that are most important to them. What do you want to do, see, and experience in the next 2, 5, or 10 years?

To answer your question, Molly— yes, I do have a Bucket List. I've completed a number of items on my list, and am saving the money I need to pursue the next activities on my list.

MPH: That's fascinating. Would you mind sharing some personal examples?

JSE: Of course—I'd be happy to share. Let's walk through some items that I recently checked off my bucket list:

Bucket List	Activities
Go on Safari	I travelled to Kenya in 2017 and visited the Masai Mara National Park, amongst many other locations.
Hot Air Balloon Flight	Whilst I was in Kenya, I decided to take an early morning trip to watch the sun rise over the savannah. The views were spectacular, and the memory of watching the animals in their natural habitat as the day broke will stay with me for many years.
Visit All the Grand Prix Races on the Calendar	I plan to visit all the Grand Prix races on the Championship calendar. This is a long-standing list item, and will take some time to complete, as it is quite expensive. I enjoy combining my holidays with Grand Prix races. Since creating my Bucket List, I've been to Grand Prix races in Bahrain, Silverstone, China, Singapore, and Abu Dhabi.
Write a Book	Here we are! If you're reading this list in your paperback or on your e-reader, then this book will have been published in Q4 2018.
Encourage People to Be the Best They Can Be	I run a webpage that shares inspirational quotes and messages for a community of over 2,000 people. Also, I run an F1 page to enable people to keep up to speed on F1 news. This book is about surviving F1 withdrawal by encouraging people to experiment and be the best that they can be – A hybrid of the two.

MPH: Wow, that's impressive. I'm on it. I understand what you mean, and I agree that the years seem to fly by. There are many things that I want to achieve, but before I know it, its New Year's again, and I make the same commitments! I need to break the cycle. Could you share more thoughts or examples to help people achieve their Bucket List goals?

JSE: Yes, of course. Here's a list of 50 activities to get people thinking about their goals. The important thing is to not simply select items from the list, but to take a moment to step back and think about what you enjoy and what you really want to do.

Abseiling	Cooking	Investing in Stocks	Masters/ PhD	Snorkelling
Random Acts of Kindness	Visit Empire State Building	Learn to Juggle	See the Northern Lights	Start a Business
Adopt an Animal	Visit Glastonbury	Karaoke	Paint	Swim with Dolphins
Archery	Gondola Ride	Learn to Knit	Paraglide	Visit Sydney Opera House
Visit Buckingham Palace	Visit Great Barrier Reef	Kung Fu	See the Pyramids	Try Tandem Skydiving
Visit Burj Khalifa	Visit Grand Canyon	Learn Guitar	Road Trip	Gain a Toned Body
Go Camping	Horse Riding	Learn Piano	Scuba Dive	Complete a Triathlon
Learn to Play Chess / Draughts	Hot Air Balloon	Visit the Louvre	Go Skiing	Volunteer
Climb a Mountain	Visit an Ice Hotel	See Machu Picchu	Sky Dive	Write a Book
Go to a Concert	Reach Ideal Weight	Run a Marathon	Sleep in the Desert	Yoga

Note anything that comes to mind. Don't let practicalities or self-doubt stop the flow. Write from your heart—what do you want? Don't consider what your partner, husband, wife, children, parents, dog, cat, or flowers want—what do **YOU** want?

Remember the safety briefing, on an aircraft, who's oxygen mask, do you put on first? **YOURS!** This is about **YOU.**

I know that I'm not Aladdin, but imagine that the genie and the lamp are here. What are your wishes?

Once you have made your list, the next step is to visualise what needs to happen to make the completion of your list items a reality. Imagine yourself achieving your goals. If a list item requires funding, then start saving. Put the plans in place to make your dreams a reality.

A wish list is exactly that—your dreams may never happen unless you act to make them a reality. If you fail to do so, your dreams are just another piece of paper hidden away in an already-full drawer. So, act—do it NOW! This is your life. Be truly happy with it.

Chapter Eight: Box, Box, Box – Pit Lane Time

Everybody laughs in the same language.

Anonymous

MPH: I'm very energised by the last chapter. I think you may be changing the pace now—is that correct?

JSE: It is, indeed. However, there is still plenty to be excited about! There will be a change in intensity from the last chapter.

You can almost switch your brain off in this chapter after the last one—but not quite! Some may still find this chapter a challenge.

MPH: OK, I'm intrigued – what's "box, box, box" all about?

JSE: Well, Molly, we've discussed a few times today how hectic life can be at times, and that sometimes you simply need to relax and take a bit of a time-out.

This time-out could be a weekend, or perhaps a bank holiday or national day celebration, depending on the customs of your home country.

Box, box, box is simply about taking that time—closing the door, putting on your comfy clothes (or even PJs), grabbing your favourite food, and escaping into the world of the box set or TV Series.

MPH: I can definitely do this one!

JSE: Absolutely. We've all been there. The biggest challenge is when you finish one episode, and it's a cliff hanger, so you think, OK, one more, then another, and before you know it, it's 2AM and you need to be up for work soon!

MPH: (Laughs) I'm laughing because it's so true.

JSE: I'm guilty as charged, also, which is why a long weekend is perfect—you don't need to face the commute, the drive, or the workplace whilst you're tired from a long night.

That's the key. Schedule some time for yourself, or just be spontaneous. Close that door, and temporarily switch off the world to have some chill time.

MPH: I like this. So, what are your recommendations?

JSE: OK, sure. So, speaking purely from my own experience, these are some box sets / TV Sets that I'd recommend for someone who wants to escape the world.

I'm sure that there are many more available that I haven't yet seen, so please feel free to explore and do your own research. This is based upon my own experience.

My recommendations, in no particular order, are as follows:

- Designated Survivor
- The Bodyguard
- Game of Thrones
- 24
- Blue Planet
- Line of Duty
- Breaking Bad
- Downton Abbey
- Elementary
- Orange is the New Black

- Suits
- Grey's Anatomy
- Happy Valley
- Homeland
- House of Cards
- Peaky Blinders
- Planet Earth
- Friends
- Pride and Prejudice
- The Wire
- True Blood

There you go—kick back and enjoy!

Chapter Nine: The World: Where Will You Go?

Travel is the only thing you buy that makes you richer.

Anonymous

JSE: Let's move on from our discussion of chilled-out box set binges and go travel the world!

MPH: Sounds good to me—I'm in!

JSE: We touched on travelling earlier when we discussed our Bucket Lists. Many people like to travel. Why? Why do you think it's so popular?

MPH: Perhaps a chance to get away? To explore something new?

JSE: Yes, absolutely. A scientific study has suggested that over 80% of people experience a dramatic improvement in emotional and mental wellbeing after just 48 hours on holiday.

MPH: I can definitely agree with that. What have your experiences taught you about travelling?

JSE: Travelling is very important to me. I switch off from work and just immerse myself in wherever I've travelled, even if that means simply relaxing with a drink and watching the world go by.

I really enjoy just getting out of my usual routine. In response to your question, Molly, in my opinion, the top five benefits of traveling are:

- Learning about and experiencing a different culture—getting out and sightseeing. I like to learn, see new things, and appreciate and understand a different way of being or living. The sights, smells, sounds, and colours of different places fascinate me. I enjoy meeting new people, both locals and travellers alike.

  I truly believe that travel broadens the mind and helps you to truly embrace diversity and appreciate our differences across cultures.

  Relaxing, catching up on news and books, and expanding my mind. Often, at work, when you're preparing to go on leave, things become more intense than usual, and its therefore not uncommon to be behind on news or to have neglected your to-read pile.

  I like to use my brain, and to understand the latest developments in F1 or other news. I usually catch up on this whilst traveling, or in the first few days of holiday.

- Experiencing the local foods, flavours, and smells. We discussed my love of food earlier. Immersing yourself and experimenting with the local foods is good fun. In Thailand, for instance, we took a cooking class to learn how to make some popular Thai dishes. I remember that some locals gathered to watch us, and they were impressed that we wanted to understand their culture and learn to make some local dishes. Naturally, we were able to share our new skills and the recipes we learned with our family and friends.

- Pressing the reset button. I like the freedom to do nothing or everything. This is something I would encourage everyone to do. Just press the reset button, and take time out to just *be*. Reflect on your life (you don't need to be too deep!), and perhaps even dig out your Bucket List and think about what's next for you. This gives you something positive to focus upon when you've returned home and are back in your daily routine - Perhaps, even facing those holiday blues.

- Enhancing your resilience. With travel comes adventure, and things will inevitably happen that you haven't expected (my experience in China immediately springs to mind!). The more you travel, the more you're able to deal with these situations and to build the skills and coping mechanisms that will help you to deal with almost any eventuality with minimal stress. You learn to take challenges in your stride.

MPH: That's really interesting. So, we've explored some of the benefits of travel, and your own personal experiences. Where should we consider visiting?

JSE: Now that really is the money question, Molly. The world is your oyster—you can go anywhere you want to go, and do anything you want to do.

It all comes down to what you enjoy doing, your budget, and whether you're adventurous or want to be glued to a sunbed for the duration of your holiday.

I mentioned earlier that I like to combine Grand Prix races with my holidays, so those destinations are always on my map to be explored! Let's look at some popular destinations and things that you can explore there to give fans some ideas and to whet their appetites:

- Snorkelling in Mauritius
- Visiting the Pyramids in Egypt
- Experiencing the Singapore Sling in Raffles, Singapore
- Staying in an Eco-Lodge in Greenland
- Going on Safari in Kenya
- Meandering Las Ramblas in Barcelona, Spain
- Riding in a Tuk-Tuk in Bangkok
- Catching a Show on the Strip in Las Vegas, United States

- Swimming with Dolphins in Mexico
- Visiting the Rice Fields of Bali
- Tobogganing the Great Wall of China
- Walking the Circuit in Monaco
- Seeing the Eiffel Tower and the Mona Lisa in Paris, France
- Riding a Gondola in Venice, Italy
- Visiting Burj Khalifa and Exploring the Desert in Dubai, UAE
- Seeing the Oriental Pearl Tower in Shanghai, China
- Visiting the Colosseum in Rome, Italy
- Seeing Victoria Harbour in Hong Kong
- Wandering Times Square in New York City, United States
- Visiting Buckingham Palace in London, England
- Seeing the Tower of Pisa in Pisa, Italy
- Visiting the Forbidden City in Beijing, China
- Exploring Disneyland in Florida, United States
- Seeing an Opera in the Sydney Opera House in Sydney, Australia
- Climbing Mount Everest in Nepal and Tibet
- Visiting the Ruins in Petra, Jordan
- Seeing the Terra Cotta Warriors in Xian, China
- Visiting Penguin Island in Perth, Australia
- Climbing Mount Kilimanjaro in Tanzania
- Seeing Red Square in Moscow, Russia
- Visiting the Taj Mahal in India
- Seeing the Meiji Shrine in Tokyo, Japan
- Climbing Table Mountain in Cape Town, South Africa
- Seeing Niagara Falls in Ontario, Canada
- Wandering the Acropolis in Athens, Greece
- Snorkelling the Great Barrier Reef in Queensland, Australia

- Visiting Machu Picchu in Peru
- Seeing the Northern Lights in Highlands, Iceland
- Visiting Kuala Lumpur, Malaysia
- Seeing Ha Long Bay, Vietnam

MPH: Thanks. And we should presumably include all F1 circuit locations in our lists.

JSE: Absolutely. Why not? It would be rude not to.

Chapter Ten: Charge the Engine Control Unit (ECU)

If you only look at what is, you may never attain what could be.

Anonymous

MPH: OK, so this chapter intrigues me. I have to ask—what's the "ECU," and what is this chapter all about?

JSE: (Laughs) Sorry, Molly, I like to keep you on your toes. It is a curious title, in all fairness. Let's deal with the Engine Control Unit (ECU) first. The ECU is essentially the brain of the F1 car. It's a powerful computer that controls everything within the car. The ECU processes and transmits massive quantities of information and data to the engineers regarding the performance of the car.

The purpose of this chapter is to think about charging our brains—feeding them, if you like, with information that helps us to remain current from a performance perspective, just like F1 cars.

MPH: OK, that makes sense. How do you do this?

JSE: I charge my brain by reading and by learning languages. I'm far from fluent in these languages, don't get me wrong, but I do enjoy learning. So, you may be thinking—why should you charge your brain? You may secretly be wishing that you were back in Chapter 8, immersed in a box set.

It's a fair question, so let's consider the benefits and kick it around a little. For example, how many languages do you think are spoken around the world?

MPH: I honestly don't know—perhaps 200?

JSE: I originally thought that, as well, but its estimated that there are between 6,500 and 7,000 languages spoken around the world! In fairness, approximately a third of those languages are spoken by only about 1,000 people.

MPH: Wow! That's a surprise. I didn't expect the number to be that large. There must be some languages that dominate?

JSE: Absolutely—you're right. The ten languages that are most frequently spoken are:

- Chinese (Mandarin)
- Spanish
- English
- Hindi
- Arabic
- Portuguese
- Bengali
- Russian
- Japanese
- Punjabi / Lahnda

Interestingly, some organisations recognise "official" business languages. Take the United Nations, for example, which conducts business in English, French, Spanish, Chinese, Russian, and Arabic.

MPH: That's really interesting, and makes sense. I do like the idea of learning a language, but to be honest, I'm apprehensive that I would mess it up! I know that you've worked abroad—have you experienced that?

JSE: That makes sense. I've definitely experienced that myself. I think that it's important to push through and try anyway. What's the worst that could happen? Maybe you won't be understood, and must be more creative as you ask your question.

In my experience, learning a language really does feed the brain. Problem solving, memory, concentration, and multi-tasking are all skills that I have I've learned or used in my language training.

There are other benefits of learning another language, too. I was discussing this with some friends last week. They have found that learning new languages has helped them to make connections and friends, to advance their careers, and even to increase their confidence.

I believe that language learning enables you to genuinely immerse yourself in a different culture. You can see things from a different perspective, and can better recognise and celebrate cultural differences.

MPH: Recognise and celebrate cultural differences—I really like that. It would really help on holidays, to be fair.

JSE: Exactly. That's how I think of it. Differences are just different, not right or wrong, good or bad. We're simply different because of our histories, and our cultural evolution over the years. Even if you just try the basics, like "hello," "how are you," "please," and "thank you," it makes a huge difference. Just go for it.

MPH: I will try!

JSE: OK, but what's stopping you? I can tell from your body language that you're thinking, "Hmm, it's something I'd like to do, but I don't think that I will!"

MPH: Wow! How did you know? That's actually quite impressive. I was thinking that the problem is time—it's finding the time. I like reading, and I like to learn. It's always something I intend to do, but in truth, I never do. How did you do it?

JSE: That's a really good point, Molly. You're definitely not alone! I stumbled across my solution by accident, to be honest.

I was taking a course at work, and one of the subjects that we covered was time management. In one exercise, we detailed how we spent our time in any given week.

I discovered that I spent 8 hours and 20 minutes each week in my car on my commute to work (50 mins each way per day). It actually was a shock! It really shouldn't have been a shock, but I just hadn't thought about it. 8 hours and 20 minutes a week. Let's say that four weeks I was on leave or visiting different sites. That's 48 weeks of commuting—24,000 minutes a year, or 400 hours!

What could you do with 400 hours? At the time, I was just listening to the local radio and making a few hands-free calls—that was it. I decided to listen to one audiobook each week.

I mix it up a little by listening to the radio sometimes, and other times listening to books. I started learning Spanish, and then moved on to other books. Some are work-related, and some are autobiographies—whatever I feel like. I find that I'm more refreshed when I get home when I listen to audiobooks whilst driving.

MPH: I can't believe that my commute is approximately 30 minutes per day, or 15 minutes each way. I've never thought about that, either. As you rightly say, those minutes add up. That's really insightful, and I need to think about that. I definitely want to maximise that time. Thank you!

JSE: You're very welcome. My pleasure.

Chapter Eleven: Clear the Garage

Organise your life around your dreams and watch them come true.

Anonymous

JSE: So—when I say "clear the garage," are you thinking, *what is this all about?*

MPH: I am! I'm also still in shock at the hours I spend commuting!

JSE: Sure, I understand. So, think about the "pit walk" for a second— what do you notice in every driver's garage as you walk through?

MPH: I'm not sure—it's always very clean.

JSE: Yes, it is. Each constructor has a system. Well-organised and often lean methodologies are used to maximise the space and to ensure that items can be sourced quickly and efficiently. It's certainly not cluttered! Often, you'll notice that parts, equipment, and even tyres are labelled for each of the drivers.

MPH: Yes, I have noticed that.

JSE: This chapter is inspired by the pit walk—it's all about decluttering.

MPH: Oh OK. I certainly need to listen carefully, then. Decluttering has been on my To Do list since the school holidays, I'm ashamed to say!

JSE: Well, I know from experience, Molly, that you are most definitely not alone! It's often something we say that we will "get around to," and somehow, someway, something always happens or gets in the way of completing it.

I must confess that I've got a bit of OCD, so it's actually something that I really enjoy.

MPH: What advice would you give to F1 fans on this issue? Why declutter, where to start, what to do, and what do you actually mean by "decluttering"?

JSE: All good questions, Molly. By "decluttering," I mean that you should declutter your life, but if that sounds way too scary, then don't worry! Start small and work your way up.

That's a key piece of advice not only for this chapter, but for all the chapters in this book. You can simply do as much or as little as you find possible. What works for you should always be your focus.

I understand that decluttering every aspect of your life may sound dramatic, but it's one option that's open to you. By "life," I don't mean a life sentence! I mean your house or apartment (yes the "rubbish drawer" is included), your car (if you drive), your workspace (or your bedroom for our younger fans!), your computer, tablet, and mobile phone, your routine, or even your friends.

MPH: Oh, wow—I've never thought about decluttering devices or friends, to be honest. I just have palpitations thinking about decluttering the garage or the "rubbish drawer"!

JSE: Sure, I can relate. I used to think exactly the same way many years ago. Then, out of sheer boredom and a new job that required me to move house, I changed my ways. I can say from experience that I am not someone who tends to hoard things or buy in excess, but seriously, I could not believe just how much junk I had—things I hadn't used in years! Not to mention the rubbish drawer (or cupboard)—you know we all have one! Be honest.

MPH: Guilty as charged! I do have one, actually—it's just convenient. You may be in a rush, or someone pops around, and you think, *Oh, clear the decks!* In it goes.

JSE: I know, it's true. You're absolutely right. Next, let's explore the many studies that have been undertaken over the years that show the benefits of decluttering. These benefits include feeling less stress, feeling in control of your life, spending less time doing or looking for things, and a sense of feeling renewed and refreshed.

MPH: Yes, I can imagine that—I've just never experienced it.

JSE: Of course. Well, you can experience it, and if you make the time, you will! It's that simple. Let's start by exploring each area in more depth, and I'll take you through my experiences.

MPH: I'm listening, and I will make the time—I promise!

JSE: OK good. Please do something for me—do it only for yourself. Don't do it because you feel in some way obligated because of this discussion. I want you and every other F1 fan to be happy and to live the life you want to live.

MPH: I will. You're right. I just need to stop thinking and start doing! What has worked for you?

JSE: Before we get started, there are two things I want to share that I always remember whilst decluttering.

Firstly, "everything has a place, and everything in its place." My gran used to use this phrase when my brother and I were children, as we would naturally cause chaos with all our toys whilst on visits! My mum frequently uses this phrase, also. This, amongst many other good principles, has been instilled in us all.

Secondly, as I've grown older and faced some of life's challenges, I find myself thinking, *collect memories, not things.* Spending time with people I care about, doing things I've always wanted to do, and having Bucket List experiences means more to me than buying things.

Don't get me wrong—there must be a balance, and it's good to have physical things to remind us of our memories. But give me a choice and make me choose, and I would choose experiences and memories every single time.

MPH: I couldn't agree more. That connects with what you said earlier about people with terminal illness—I'm sure they didn't say, "I wish I had more clutter or things in my life!"

JSE: You're absolutely right, Molly. Let's take each in turn, and I'll walk you through what always works for me. I try to declutter twice per year, in the F1 summer break and at the end of the Championship. At the very least, I declutter once a year, just to keep on top of things, both mentally and physically. Let's go!

House, Apartment, or Bedroom

Mental State:

1) I'm moving house.
2) Anything that irritates me or is broken is going to be sorted.
3) Anything that I haven't used in the last six to twelve months is leaving the house.

How To:

1) Three Piles for Any Activity:

   a. KEEP – To be kept and put in its rightful place (remember my Gran's words).
   b. SELL OR DONATE - To be sold, given away, or donated to charity.
   c. GONE – To be thrown away, as it's no longer required.

2) Anything that is broken or needs replacing will be sorted and finished before I start decluttering another room.

Rules:

1) Start Small: Start with the smallest or least cluttered room in your house to gain your circuit prowess.

2) One Room at a Time: Declutter one room or area of your life at a time, and finish decluttering within the same day. If you think, "I'm really in the mood," don't start another room unless you know that you have the energy to finish it (even if it means a 2AM finish!), even if it takes you the entire 15 weeks to complete the decluttering task! I usually aim to declutter one room per night every other weekday, and leave any big rooms (or the garage) until the weekend.

3) Donate Often: "I'll keep it, it may come in handy" is a dangerous phrase. Red flags are out! Add these items to your donation pile and give them to someone who can really make use of them, rather than allowing it to take up valuable space in your home.

4) Move at Pace: Do not overthink the process. Go with your instinct and crack on.

5) Recycle: Wherever possible, recycle rather than trash. It is our planet, after all.

MPH: I love it. When you break it down like that, there really is no reason to not declutter.

JSE: Exactly, Molly—sometimes we all just need a little nudge. It's really not difficult. It's actually quite therapeutic, once you get started. I work my way through the house, usually starting with the bathroom! So, go for it.

MPH: I could do that later—that shouldn't take long at all.

JSE: That's the spirit, Molly. Let's continue.

Wardrobe

The "Mental State" and "How To" rules remain unchanged in this section.

Rules:

1) If I haven't worn it in six months, it should be donated or thrown away.

2) If it doesn't fit anymore (too big or too small), it should be donated or thrown away. Exception: I am on a mission to lose or gain weight, therefore, I'm going to choose my favourite item (or pin a photo of me wearing it) and put it in a visible place. Every day, I'm going to see it, so that it becomes my motivation.

3) My footwear and coats are included in this process.

Car

Mental State:

1) I've sold my car, and it's going next Saturday.
2) I get my new car next Saturday.

The "How To" rules remain unchanged in this section.

Rules:

1) I'm going to be really thorough and check every pocket and under all the mats.

2) I'm going to clean the car or take it to be cleaned inside and out.

3) I'm going to check or have a mechanic check the oil, water, and tyres.

MPH: OK, this is really working for me. I sat here thinking, OK, that's easy. It sounds so simple when you break it down in that way.

JSE: It is! Honestly. I always feel great when I declutter. The reason I suggest that you finish a room or area before moving on to the next is simply that I want you to feel that sense of achievement. You will systematically work through the house. The "done" rooms become a feel-good factor and an inspiration, as does the volume of things you plan to donate or throw away. Any items that you decide to sell become a bonus and a funding stream for your new household items, clothes, car gadgets, and extra cash!

Workspace

Dependent upon your workspace, this may take seconds, minutes, or hours! In this example, I'm decluttering an office.

Mental State:

1) I've got the desk I always wanted near the window.
2) I move to a new desk tomorrow!

If you don't have a clear-desk policy, add some photos of your family, pets, or F1 cars. Ensure that these photos represent their subjects as they are today!

Be honest! Do you find yourself saying, "Oh yes, they are my children, but actually, they're 8 and 10 years old now," only to be looking at photos in which they were toddlers? Fix it!

The "Mental State" and "How To" rules remain unchanged in this section.

MPH: That's so true—my colleague does that. Her photographs must be at least five years out of date.

JSE: It doesn't surprise me, to be honest. Our lives are so busy! We are creatures of habit.

Mobile, Computer, and Other Devices

Mental State:

1) My device is running slowly due to the number of files or apps.
2) I may need to upgrade my device, but with a smaller memory capacity.

How To:

1) I'm going consider all my apps, programmes, and files, and delete any that I no longer use.
2) I'm going to ensure that I have the latest updates on all apps, programmes, and operating systems.
3) I'm going to delete any contacts I no longer need, or ensure that all contact information is up to date (including addresses!). Hopefully, these will be minor tweaks to the information of people who may have moved recently, and you're not starting a few decades ago.
4) I'm going to review the latest apps to see if there's anything that will help me stay organised.
5) I'm going to review and cull my e-mail.
6) I'm going to organise all my photographs.

Rules:

1) Start Small: Start with the smallest folders to gain your momentum.

2) One Folder or Group at a Time: Undertake one folder or group at a time, and finish that task before moving on.

3) As with the house, the phrase, "I'll keep it, it may come in handy" is too dangerous. Red flags are out! Be bold, and hit that delete key.

4) Move at Pace: Don't overthink it. Go with your instinct, and systematically move through the rest of the files.

5) Back Up: Ensure all back up settings are up-to-date, and that a back-up occurs automatically on a regular basis to maintain all your documents.

MPH: OK. I'm feeling slightly guilty now, but I know that it needs to be done!

JSE: That's OK, Molly. Take your phone, for example. This is one of the things you can do on your commute by train, bus, or aircraft. Just start to work through the guidance offered above. Even if you only spend minutes per day, you're making progress.

Friends

For some people, this is uncomfortable. So, I'm just going to put it out there for you to think about. There are no rules with this one—it's simply meant to encourage you to think about the fact that this is your life, time, and headspace.

Earlier today, we discussed various activities, including the Bucket List, which includes things you want to do in your life. Do you ever find yourself saying, "I never have the time?"

Do you ever find yourself making excuses when invited to meet certain friends? Perhaps you experience a physical aversion when they offer to "pop around and visit." If you do, I encourage you to consider why.

I'm not saying that you should ditch all your friends and start again—absolutely not. Everyone goes through tough times, and being there for each other is important.

But I do suggest that you reflect on *why*. Life simply takes its course, and you may find that over several years, you've grown apart, you no longer have anything in common, or perhaps someone is incredibly negative about everything and everybody. This type of friendship can become draining and can feel toxic.

So, reflect and make a conscious choice about how you spend your time, and with whom. If you find yourself in the "I never have time" camp, then create time.

MPH: You're right—I felt slightly uneasy just now, but that may be because it's a topic we don't often discuss. I can immediately think of one person who I do find myself making excuses not to see, and I really have to be in the right mood to spend time with her.

JSE: Sure, I can appreciate that, and I think you're right. In my experience, you don't need to spend valuable time analysing why or what's gone wrong or approaching the individual to explain. Those are all logical thoughts. However, recognising that we are all different may prompt unintended consequences should you decide to take that route. I would simply encourage fans to be conscious of it, and to make yourself less available. There is no need to be innovative with excuses or even to lie (even white lies!)—just say it as it is, "I can't make it," "I'm busy," or "No thank you, that doesn't interest me." Often, we find it difficult to just say no! You may find that, over time, the invitations may slacken and eventually cease.

MPH: Thank you. I appreciate that clarification. If I think of my own experience, friends have come in and out of my life, and there hasn't been any drama or awkward discussions. It's just happened.

JSE: Exactly! It is your life. Your time. Your bucket list and your dreams. I'm simply asking you to stay focussed on your journey, and to refuse to take diversions that you don't want to take. Does that make sense?

MPH: Yes, I like that analogy.

Chapter Twelve: Design and Develop Those Upgrades

Just when the caterpillar thought the world was ending, it became a butterfly.

English Proverb

MPH: OK, so now we're moving onto the next subject—"upgrades." Can you explain a little more about this, and bring the concept to life with some examples?

JSE: Of course. So far, we've considered a number of areas of our lives, including feeding and nurturing our brains (Chapter 10), our food choices (Chapter 6), improving our environment and living space (Chapter 11), and focussing on our dreams and Bucket List (Chapter 7). In the high-octane world of F1, being the best constructor or driver is a constant area of focus.

F1 teams work hard throughout the year, constantly looking for innovative ways to drive performance and improvements to their cars. Similarly, the drivers take the same approach with their fitness regimes and diet, continually striving for the marginal improvements that make all the difference.

So, my question to all fans is this. In order to be the best that you can possibly be as a person, what should be your focus? We're all different, which is what makes this planet such an interesting and diverse place to live!

You may wish to kick a particular habit, or conversely, to learn a new skill. To answer your earlier question, Molly, some examples of "upgrades" include:

Upgrades : Potential Overrides	Upgrades : Potential New Releases
Give up or limit chocolate	Learn the guitar
Reduce amount of time spent gaming	Drink more water
Quit smoking	Meditate
Stop hitting the snooze button	Get more sleep
Reduce fast food intake	Improve your food choices
Stop surrounding yourself with negative people	Perform random acts of kindness

MPH: Thanks! So, what are the key steps you recommend that fans implement to be successful?

JSE: Good question, Molly. Here are the five key steps that I implement to achieve my goals:

- **STEP 1: Decide and Call It** – Take a little time to think about the things that you'd like to improve, or that frustrate you. Alternatively, consider what you've always wanted to do. Simply decide, and make that personal commitment.

- **STEP 2: Make It Public** – Once you've decided, tell your friends, family, and work colleagues about your decision. By doing this, you'll give yourself the motivation to succeed and to inspire others. Simply knowing that others may be watching can sometimes be enough to ensure that you don't deviate from your goals.

- **STEP 3: Focus on the Chequered Flag** – Keep your focus, and visualise yourself living the life you want, having already achieved your goals.

- **STEP 4: Self-Talk and Engage Your Race Engineer** – Keep your thoughts and narrative positive about your upgrade choices. At the start of the process, identify a close friend or partner to be your race engineer. If you encounter any challenges in your journey, talk it through with your engineer, and agree on the tactics you should use to remain focussed and win the race.

- **STEP 5: Battles, Wars, and Incentives** – As your upgrades take shape, you may experience a malfunction—you may lose or need to concede a battle. Take a deep breath and remain focussed on the war. Just because you've gone outside of the track limits doesn't mean that you're out of the race. Stay true to yourself, and charge your courage and strength by following Step 4.
  - Set targets, and when you reach them, reward yourself! It's always a good idea to have a visual narrative of your progress. If your upgrade involves saving money (quitting smoking, for example), save the cash you'd normally spend in a jar and treat yourself when you reach your targets. Similarly, photographs and visualisation techniques are also useful prompts. Ensure that you place these prompts in a prominent place (on the bathroom mirror or the fridge, for example).

MPH: Thank you. I really like the steps you've just taken us through. You make things easy to understand and implement.

This and many of other chapters have inspired me—I just want to get started and, as you've said throughout, take some action.

JSE: Thanks Molly—that's very kind. I appreciate that.

In fact, I'm going to demonstrate Step 2 for you right now. I'm going to declare my commitment to do something I've always wanted to—I'm going to learn to play the guitar.

MPH: Oh wow! Is that an exclusive?

JSE: (Laughs) Absolutely, Molly—you heard it here first.

MPH: Excellent! We wish you the very best of luck, and look forward to hearing about your progress. Two quick questions—is this an item on your Bucket List? And who's your race engineer?

JSE: (Laughs) You are getting to know me well, Molly. Yes, it is on my Bucket List. In terms of my race engineer, I'll have to discuss that with her first, as she's also the race engineer for this book! She's immensely supportive but equally keeps me on the pit straight (and narrow).

Chapter Thirteen: Other Interesting Stuff

MPH: I believe that we are going to change gears now, and do things a little differently. Could you outline this for us?

JSE: Yes, of course. Unfortunately, we've reached the finale of our discussion, so I thought we'd mix it up a little, and follow the same format as qualifying.

Therefore, here, you'll find shorter overviews of techniques to try as you push through the pit wall to be the best that you can possibly be.

Qualifying Preparation: The Rhythm of Life

You don't get harmony when everybody sings the same note.

Anonymous

What's It All About?

Music—it provides the rhythm of life. Many studies over the years have shown the benefits of music to people's mood. For as long as I can remember, music has been a constant in my life—from nursery rhymes to contemporary music!

I've always been fascinated by how listening to a certain song can transport you in time through your memory. It can evoke emotions that stimulate dopamine levels, and result in that feel-good factor. Conversely, music can also bring comfort in the most challenging of circumstances.

I would often play music whilst I was volunteering that would enable patients to enjoy their favourite songs and even reconnect with the world—especially patients with Alzheimer's. Just seeing one smile would make that day memorable and worthwhile.

Hints and Tips

- Develop a playlist for each circuit. Think about the country, the music, and the sounds of the nation. Be creative and make it authentic.
- Develop a playlist for the main acts who have supported the concerts for the race weekend. For example, the 2018 playlist would include Guns N Roses and Sam Smith, who supported the Abu Dhabi Grand Prix.
- Develop a playlist to match your mood:

  o Celebration Playlist
  o The World Is Unfair Playlist (we've just had a DNF due to a technical issue)
  o Feel Good Playlist (for your journey to the circuit)

- Dance! This connects with our discussion in Chapter 5, as it's a great way to keep fit! Irrespective of the outcome of the race, if things are going your way, you may feel the urge to throw some shapes on the dance floor (lounge or armchair). Just go for it, and dance like you've never danced before—enjoy. Worried about your neighbours? Don't be. Simply close the curtains, blinds, or shutters, and do your thing.

Q1: Breathe that Clear Air!

When you own your breath, nobody can steal your peace.

Anonymous

What's it All About?

Gardening and meditation! Breathe in through your nose, hold for five seconds, breathe out through your mouth, and relax. Breathe it in, and get that clear air!

We could take some inspiration here from Jim Clark— a bit of farming, perhaps? Below are some ideas from my own experience.

Hints and Tips

- Apply the F1 theme to your garden.

  o Make the best use of the downforce whilst mowing the lawn.

  o Choose your colours well. If Lewis is your man, you could go with a red, white, and blue theme for your plants and flowers to represent the British flag.

  o Obtain some old tyres, clean them up, and paint them in various bright colours. Either use these as large planters, or as seats, as they do in the Bahrain Grand Prix.

  o Replicate the black and white edging of the track in your garden.

- Grow your own herbs, fruits, and vegetables.

  o Build a veggie patch. I built a small wooden veggie patch when I first started out. I grew peppers, carrots, lettuce, cucumbers, potatoes (in black bags!) and even a pumpkin one year. It's very easy, and there is something very rewarding about heading out into the garden and returning with the fresh ingredients that you've just picked.

- No garden or room to grow? You can still feel the benefits of a garden from a humble plant. Simply buy a plant and nurture it. Watch it flourish as it grows under your care.

- In our ever-changing world, the ability to access information through social media has become instantaneous. So why step out? Meditation and mindfulness techniques have been proven to provide a number of benefits, including reduced blood pressure, improved sleep, and reduced stress and anxiety levels. There are a number of excellent apps available to support your mindfulness. Headspace and Mindfulness are two free apps that I use for this purpose.

Q2: Championship – Calling All Drivers

Attitudes are contagious. Is yours worth catching?

Anonymous

What's It All About?

This is pure indulgence! A healthy competition with friends and families to host an F1 Championship will prepare you for the season ahead.

Hints and Tips

- Get Prepared – Develop a scoreboard for the event to capture scores as you race through the various events. You may decide to add other activities or bonus points in addition to the core game.

- Test Your Food Choices – In Chapter 6, we explored food choices. You can use this time and your select group of drivers to experiment with your choice of nourishment and snacks ahead of the actual season, before watching the first race in Melbourne.

- Agree Upon the Prizes in Advance – You can have as much fun with this step as you like, including offering a wooden spoon as the Worst Driver Award. You may decide to simply give three trophies, and make this an annual event.

- Create a Fantasy League – Carry on the adrenaline from your event into the season as you develop your own bespoke league. There are many sites on which you can develop a fantasy league at no cost. Alternatively, you can always like a Facebook group and join their fantasy Grand Prix league to add a further level of competitiveness (i.e. F1 Pit Board https://www.facebook.com/F1FansPitBoard/).

- Start a Blog or Create a Webpage – Alternatively, you may decide to create a blog or webpage to promote discussion during the races or to share F1 news and information, effectively creating your own community, either locally or globally.

Q3: Pole Pre-Season Essentials

Organising is a journey, not a destination.

Anonymous

<u>What's It All About?</u>

Ensure that you're organised and ready for the F1 season, including preparing your food provisions and saving those all-important dates!

<u>Hints and Tips</u>

- Lock in Grand Prix Dates – The most important task is to obtain these dates for the year ahead, and to lock them into your calendar (both Personal and Work). Do it now!
- Key Events – If you're aware of any upcoming weddings or birthdays, ensure that you contact the event planners early to influence the dates (if possible) before they are confirmed. If there are any births due, check the due dates and the local Wi-Fi coverage of the race location.
- Merchandise – Are you season-ready? Do you have your new team shirt? Wear those colours with pride! Check out the pre-season sales.
- Food Provisions – OK, this is your final task. You may wish to do this with a couple of friends to make it more competitive. Secure all your drinks, snacks, and fresh food to make your food choices secure during the race.

  o First, select your trolley or cart very carefully. Check the wheels, looking for any debris that could interfere with performance.
  o Once you're comfortable, go for it—one full circuit of the supermarket.
  o The first to reach the check-out wins.
  o Go, go, go, follow that racing line.

- Only one question remains—who's on pole?

Chapter Fourteen: Successfully Surviving Formula One Withdrawal

Someday is not a day of the week.

Anonymous

MPH: (Laughs) I like the racing line in the supermarket. I have a vision of people charging around the store.

JSE: Why not? It's a bit of fun.

MPH: I know that we're reaching the end of our interview. There are a few questions I wanted to ask in closing. What is the primary mistake that Formula One fans make that costs them time and wasted effort?

JSE: I'd have to say that it's not taking action. People always have good intentions and genuinely want to act, and may even make a solid and heartfelt commitment. For example, they may say, "I'll start my exercises on Monday after our holiday." Monday comes and goes, and there's no action, and no follow-through or delivery on the commitment.

It is human nature to want the best circumstances to start an activity. In my experience, the perfect circumstances will never occur, so just start today.

Do it now! Start the process of embedding the task into your routine as soon as possible, so that it becomes the norm.

MPH: That's true. Is there anything I haven't asked about surviving Formula One withdrawal that you'd like to share?

JSE: The final point I'd like to make is in relation to the safety car. I know that, throughout this interview, we've discussed practical techniques to deal with F1 withdrawal, and how to make it from one season to the next. We've done that in a light-hearted, engaging way.

I am conscious that, for some people, the impact of this withdrawal can be felt more acutely. Therefore, if anyone is feeling low or believes that they may have depression, please reach out. Know that people care about you, and that it's OK to feel this way. An important part of getting support is to reach out and let someone know how you're feeling. Please do that—chat with your friends and with your local doctor to understand what options are available to help you. Jump into your own safety car on that circuit, and know that we're with you every step of the way.

MPH: Of course—good point. You did say that you could be serious, and you've just proven it!

JSE: Yes, I can. I genuinely care.

Chapter Fifteen: Next Steps

One person with a belief is equal to a force of ninety-nine who only have interests.

Anonymous

MPH: Wow—we've reached our final question! I can't believe how many subjects we've covered in such a short time. This afternoon has passed so quickly. How can others find out more about what drives you, and what's next?

JSE: OK, I didn't expect that question. I created this book because I'm passionate about inspiring and motivating people to be the best that they can possibly be. That's important to me.

I wanted to share my experiences to give F1 fans greater insight into what they can do during the break, and to encourage them to think about what they want to do. Hopefully they will actively work towards realising their dreams.

In terms of what's next for me personally, we'll let the fans decide. Who knows—I may go global, or stay local—that decision is with F1 fans.

Writing this book is on my Bucket List, as is attending the F1 circuits. This book will be a funding stream to achieve the races on the calendar. I need to sell hundreds of thousands of books to make that a reality!

If I've raised one smile or helped one person to take action as a result of reading this book, then I will have achieved my purpose.

That's my real driver—to help people, and to make a difference.

Nothing makes me happier than seeing someone realise their dreams or potential.

If you've enjoyed reading this book, please let your friends, work colleagues, and family know about it, and share the love!

The final thing I'll share with you is a free gift. I'd like to build a community where people can connect, share their progress, and support each other. Therefore, head on over to join our community at http://bit.ly/f1withdrawal.

This will enable you to connect with other like-minded people and fellow F1 withdrawal survivors.

MPH: Excellent. That's great news—I'll be joining the community for sure. Thank you, J S Eton, for your time this afternoon, and thank you for sharing your experiences, tips, and techniques to survive F1 withdrawal. I hope that this will be the first of many more books.

JSE: Thank you, Molly, you're very kind and very welcome. I've enjoyed our time together. I hope that you've found this afternoon useful.

MPH: I have, indeed. I'll be buying a copy of the book—I want to jot all my notes and thoughts in it.

JSE: Excellent! I hope you enjoy. I hope that you find inspiration within these pages for many years to come.

MPH: I'm sure I will. Thank you.

OK, listeners, that concludes our interview for today. If you'd like to purchase a copy of the book, either for yourself or as a present for a fellow F1 fan, please head on over to https://amzn.to/2BH86tn. *Surviving F1 Withdrawal* is also available as an eBook.

If you would like to purchase copies of this book for your organisation, please contact Amazon directly, as discounts are available for bulk purchases. Thank you.

About J S Eton

J S Eton is an expert in surviving Formula One withdrawal whose accomplishments include:

Education:

- Master of Science in Strategic Human Resources and Development
- Associate of Science in Psychology
- Self-taught writer and web developer

Work History:

- Ten years of experience coaching, mentoring, and counselling people to overcome their greatest fears and challenges and to realise their potential
- Five years of experience volunteering to enable terminally ill children and adults to go on holiday
- Successfully developed and maintained both F1 and inspirational webpages

Awards, Titles, and Designations:

- Amazon-published author
- Self-confessed "Petrol Head"
- Experienced numerous F1 circuits around the globe

Personal Information:

- More than 2,000 followers across the globe
- An inspirational writer and coach
- Lived and worked in various countries to fuel F1 holidays
- Self-taught painter who has auctioned many paintings to raise money for charity
- Speaks five languages
- Overcame fear of 2017/2018 F1 withdrawal by developing this book
- Hopes to watch a race at every circuit on the F1 calendar (Number 1 on the Bucket List)

You need instruction and encouragement from someone who has "been there and done that," and who knows how to effectively handle F1 withdrawal.

And as you can see, J S Eton is uniquely qualified to help you understand everything you need to know about surviving F1 withdrawal from one season to the next.

Overcome your fears, and experiment with new ideas and opportunities to be the best that you can be!

Printed in Great Britain
by Amazon